D1611800

T A L E S   O F

Greek Mythology

R e t o l d   T i m e l e s s   C l a s s i c s

Perfection Learning®

Retold by L. L. Owens

Editor: Susan Sexton
Illustrator: Greg Hargreaves

Text © 1999 by Perfection Learning® Corporation.

For information, contact
Perfection Learning® Corporation,
1000 North Second Avenue, P.O. Box 500
Logan, Iowa 51546-1099.
Phone: 1-800-831-4190 • Fax: 1-712-644-2392

Paperback ISBN 0-7891-2860-8
Cover Craft® ISBN 0-7807-7854-5
Printed in the U.S.A.

4 5 6 PP 06 05 04 03

Table of Contents

Introduction

A *myth* is a traditional story. *Mythology* is the term for a whole body of myths, such as Greek mythology.

The stories of Greek mythology have captivated readers for centuries. They explain many things. They can explain the sources of common human thoughts, feelings, and struggles. And even happenings in nature. This book presents just a few of these thrilling legends.

The Romans claimed the earlier Greek myths as their own. Their tales are very similar. But they used different names for the gods and other characters.

You've probably heard variations of both Greek and Roman tales. So it can be easy to confuse them. On the next page is a handy reference. It lists each character's Greek and Roman names. And it tells a little about each character's place in mythology.

Greek Name	Roman Name	Description
Aphrodite	Venus	Goddess of love, beauty
Apollo	Sol	God of the sun, archery, music, poetry
Ares	Mars	God of war
Artemis	Diana	Goddess of the moon, hunting
Athene	Minerva	Goddess of wisdom, war, the arts
Cronus	Saturn	Lord of the universe
Demeter	Ceres	Goddess of the harvest
Dionysus	Bacchus	God of wine, vegetation
Eros	Cupid	God of love
Hades/Pluto	Dis	God of the underworld
Hephaestus	Vulcan	God of fire
Hera	Juno	Goddess of marriage
Heracles	Hercules	Mortal of superior strength
Hermes	Mercury	Messenger of the gods
Hestia	Vesta	Goddess of the hearth
Odysseus	Ulysses	Mortal of rare courage
Poseidon	Neptune	God of the sea
Rhea	Cybele	Goddess of the earth
Uranus	Coelus	God of the sky
Zeus	Jupiter	King of the gods

Enjoy the myths in this collection. And remember, there are hundreds more that are just as exciting. Have fun hunting them down!

The King of the Gods

CRONUS WAS A Titan. And he was the lord of the universe. This meant that he ruled the gods and the mortals. He had done so ever since he'd overthrown his father, Uranus. (That was an awful scene, indeed!)

When he grew older, Cronus married Rhea. He was told by the spirits that one of his own children would overthrow him. Just as he'd done to his father.

He was worried. So each time Rhea gave birth to a new child, he ate it.

"Stop that!" Rhea demanded. She had just given birth to her fifth child. And Cronus had swallowed it.

"I have no choice, Rhea," said Cronus. "Do you want me to face my ruin? Because that's what will happen. *If* I allow the children to roam the universe."

"How can you kill them?" Rhea asked. "They are your own!"

"Oh, Rhea!" cried Cronus. "I would never kill our children. Don't you know that? Besides, I couldn't. Not even if I wanted to."

"But I've watched you," Rhea said. "You've swallowed each and every one of them."

"Yes, but think about it, my dear," Cronus replied. "They are *our* children. So they are gods and goddesses. They cannot be killed."

Cronus continued. "True, I swallowed them. But they live on inside me."

Rhea felt better. But she knew that she was about to give birth again. And she couldn't bear the thought of losing another child.

Zeus Is Born

Early the next morning, Rhea traveled deep into the woods. She gave birth to Zeus— her third son. Then she gave him a kiss. She whispered, "Don't cry, darling. I'm leaving you here with the wood nymphs. They will take good care of you."

Rhea placed Zeus in a golden cradle. Then she picked up a stone and wrapped it in linen. She hurried home to Cronus.

"Here is your third son," she said. "He is strong and healthy." She didn't tell Cronus the baby's name.

"Give him to me," ordered Cronus. Rhea handed over the wrapped-up stone.

Cronus quickly swallowed the bundle. And he went about his business.

Rhea was ecstatic. When Cronus was out of earshot, she exclaimed, "It worked!" And she jumped for joy.

Rhea's Scheme

Years later, Rhea went to Zeus. She had been visiting him every week since his birth. Now he was a fine, handsome young god.

"I miss you, son," Rhea said. "I want to see you every day. Won't you come home with me?"

"Will I get to meet my father?" asked Zeus.

"Yes, you will," Rhea promised. "But we won't tell him who you are right away. You see, I have been scheming. If my plan works, you shall soon meet your brothers. And your sisters too."

"Hooray!" shouted Zeus. "I can't wait!"

That night, Rhea introduced Cronus to his son. "Meet your new cupbearer, dear," she said to her husband. "His name is Zeus."

"Hello," said Cronus.

"Hello, sir," said Zeus. He was grinning from ear to ear.

"Now, Zeus," said Rhea. "Don't you have a special drink for Cronus?"

"I do," replied Zeus. He disappeared for a moment. Then he returned. And he presented a shining silver goblet to Cronus.

"What is this?" Cronus asked.

"I made it myself. You'll love it," boasted Rhea. "It's made from the sweetest nectar in the world."

"I thought I'd tried everything," said Cronus.

"Nonsense!" cried Rhea. "There are still some things that you don't know about."

Rhea winked at Zeus as Cronus took a drink.

Instantly, Cronus began to cough. He couldn't control himself.

First, he coughed up the stone he'd swallowed years before. Then he coughed so hard that he spit out all of his children!

Out came Hestia and Demeter. Hera and Hades. And—finally—Poseidon. He was carrying his trident. And he looked angry.

"What is the meaning of all this!" screamed Cronus. He was afraid.

"I missed our children," said Rhea. "Now we can be a big, happy family."

"But you don't understand, Rhea," Cronus said. "No good can come of this."

"You're right, Father," said Poseidon. "We all hate you for what you've done to us."

"I was only trying to keep things peaceful," said Cronus weakly. He knew what was in store for him. For hadn't he been warned?

The Chosen One

"The time has come, Father," said Hestia. "You must step down."

"That's right," agreed Hades. "We've had a long time to discuss this. And we shall never respect you as our ruler."

"So we have chosen a new one," said Demeter.

"Who?" said Cronus. "Is it Hades? Or Poseidon?"

"No," answered Hera. "We have chosen Zeus."

"Zeus!" cried Cronus. Until then, he hadn't realized that Zeus was his child. "Of course! Rhea—Zeus is our third son?"

"Yes, Cronus," replied Rhea. "He is. I tricked you when he was born."

Cronus looked at his children's faces, one by one. Then he studied Rhea's face.

"I have no choice," he said at last. "Zeus shall be the king of the gods. And I shall beg my children for forgiveness."

From then on, Zeus ruled the gods. He was a wise and powerful king. And all was right with the world. Well—almost!

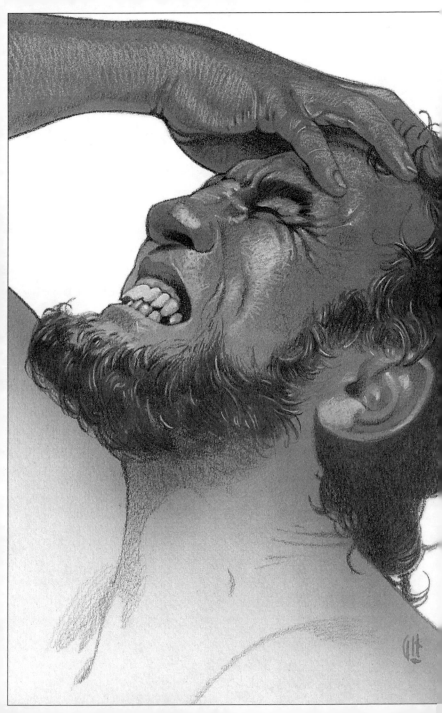

Athene and the Birth of the Spider

NOW, AS YOU know, Zeus was the king of the gods. One day, he was relaxing on Mount Olympus. Suddenly, a terrible pain seized him.

"My head!" he cried. "Quick, Hephaestus—fetch my ax!"

Hephaestus was one of Zeus's sons. "I've got it, Father!" he shouted. "What shall I do?"

"Split my head open—now!" commanded Zeus. "It's the only way!"

Well, no one disobeyed Zeus. So Hephaestus swiftly did as he was told.

And out from Zeus's head emerged a new goddess. She was beautiful. And she wore a warrior's armor.

13

"Hello, Father," she smiled. "I am Athene—goddess of wisdom, war, and the arts."

Zeus's head felt as good as new. And he was delighted to meet his new daughter. Soon, they were very close. And Athene advised Zeus on everything.

Athene had a good life. Although she was a skilled warrior, she much preferred peace. And she always tried to resolve conflict with words. She never attacked unless it was in self-defense. And she was respected for her many acts of bravery.

Among other things, Athene created the olive tree and the flute. And she taught cooking and weaving. Her talent was limitless.

But Athene had one flaw. She was terribly jealous. And this sometimes caused problems for others. What follows is perhaps the best-known story of Athene's jealousy.

❖　❖　❖

Arachne was a young peasant girl. She was a gifted weaver. People came from miles around to see her. They took great pleasure in watching her work. And even greater pleasure in seeing what she created.

One spring day, a crowd formed around Arachne. She had just won the village weaving contest. It was her fifth win in a row. A stranger asked—

"Were you taught your craft by the goddess Athene?"

"Of course not!" Arachne laughed. "Why, I've seen her tapestries. I do much better work."

The crowd gasped in horror.

"Be careful, my child," warned Arachne's mother. "You'll anger the gods."

"But, Mother," Arachne replied, "I speak the truth. My tapestries are far more beautiful than Athene's. Anyone can see that."

Just then, Athene appeared in a puff of green smoke.

"Do you challenge me, Arachne?" demanded the goddess.

"I didn't think you could hear me," replied Arachne. She was stunned.

"Then you are foolish as well as boastful," said Athene. She paced back and forth for a few moments. Then she said, "I am known for my fairness. So I will forget this matter. *If* you apologize, that is. And *if* you admit that I am the greatest weaver in the world."

"I can do neither," said Arachne. "I meant what I said."

"Very well!" roared Athene. "We shall have a contest!"

With that, she clapped her hands. Two looms appeared. And the two rivals got to work.

Arachne worked with great skill. And great speed. Her mural was beautiful. It contained many complex scenes. In each one, a god or goddess was acting a fool.

Villagers whispered among themselves. They could not believe Arachne's boldness.

"What *is* she thinking?" sighed Arachne's mother. "This will only encourage Athene's wrath."

Meanwhile, Athene's fingers flew. She wove several vivid scenes in which mortals defied the gods. In each one, the gods triumphed.

Then, to add color, she took golden rays from the sun. Silvery sparkles from the stars. Brilliant blues from the ocean. And bright splashes from spring's fresh blooms. The result was breathtaking.

Arachne saw it. And she realized that she was no match for a goddess. Silently, she slipped away from the crowd.

Athene snapped her fingers. "Judges!" she shouted. And several weavers stepped up to take a look.

One of them addressed Athene nervously. "Are we to suffer if we choose Arachne's work over yours?"

"I give you my word," Athene vowed, "you shall not suffer. I command you to vote as you see fit."

The judges studied both tapestries. Then they huddled together to vote. Finally, one judge announced—

"The winner is Athene. Never have we seen such glorious work."

"Thank you, kind judges," said Athene. "Now—where is the girl?"

"She ran away when she saw your work," said Arachne's mother.

"But why?" asked Athene.

"She was wrong," replied Arachne's mother. "And she knows that she must pay the price."

"Well, learning that lesson is punishment enough," replied Athene. "I shall not harm your daughter."

But it was too late. For Arachne had been deeply ashamed. And she had already harmed herself.

"Look over there!" cried a villager. "It's Arachne! She's hanged herself!"

The crowd turned to see the girl. She was dangling, lifeless, from the branch of an olive tree. She'd used a rope made from millions of the finest silk threads.

"My poor, poor daughter!" wailed Arachne's mother. "She was so young! And so talented!"

Athene was upset. "I would like to help," she said. "I cannot bring her back. But I can allow her to spend eternity doing what she loved most."

Athene walked over to the tree. She tapped on its trunk. And a wood nymph brought her some magic dust. Athene sprinkled the dust over Arachne's head.

Instantly, Arachne shrank to the size of a walnut. Her hair fell out. Her nose and ears disappeared. Her tiny black eyes bulged from the sides of her head. And she sprouted eight wiggly legs.

Then Athene touched the rope. It shrank into a single strand. It was so delicate that it was nearly invisible.

"It is done," declared Athene. "Arachne shall forever weave enchanting webs. She shall have no rival."

And that is how the spider came to be.

THE LABORS OF HERACLES

HERACLES WAS THE son of Zeus and a mortal woman. He was the strongest mortal who ever lived. He was even stronger than some of the gods. Even as an infant, his great strength was clear.

For example, the goddess Hera was Zeus's wife. And she just so happened to hate baby Heracles. So she sent two snakes to eat him.

But later, Hera found the child smiling and cooing in his crib. He held a strangled serpent in each hand!

As an adult, Heracles often used his strength to help others. He was very generous. And he was a loyal friend.

But sometimes, his powerful feelings overwhelmed him. And he would misuse his physical strength.

He knew better. So when his anger faded, Heracles would be ashamed. And he would punish himself.

Hera tried everything to make Heracles miserable. She even drove him insane. So much so that he killed his own wife and children.

Heracles was heartbroken when he snapped out of his madness. He asked for a severe punishment. So he was sentenced to perform a series of tasks, or *labors*. His cousin, King Eurystheus, was in charge of creating the labors.

If Heracles was successful, his crime would be forgiven. And he would be granted eternal life. Just like the gods.

Read on to find out just what Heracles had to do.

Labor 1: The Nemean Lion

First, Heracles was told to kill the Nemean lion. This was a powerful monster.

Heracles bravely entered the lion's cave. The two fought savagely. It was a bloody scene. And all the blood belonged to Heracles!

Heracles was an expert marksman. But his spears and arrows could not pierce the lion's skin. Neither could his mighty sword.

Finally, Heracles got close. He wrapped his massive hands around the lion's throat. And he strangled the last breath out of the beast.

From then on, Heracles proudly wore the lion's skin as a cape. And he wore its head as a helmet.

Labor 2: The Hydra

Next, Heracles was to destroy the Hydra. The Hydra lived in the swamps of Lerna. It had the body of a dog. And it had many heads—too many to count. (Some say there were as many as 10,000!)

But only one head held the key to the monster's life. If Heracles could chop that off, the beast would disappear forever.

Heracles swiftly lanced the Hydra's heads, a dozen at a time. But each time one head was sliced off, two more grew in its place.

At last, Heracles received a sign from Zeus. A lightning bolt pointed to the head that Heracles had to slay. But the task was going to be difficult. All the other heads twisted around to protect it.

Heracles took aim. The swirling heads were confusing him. So he closed his eyes.

In a flash, he charged at his target. He made it!

The Hydra's life-giving head fell to the ground. And the beast turned to dust.

Labor 3: The Ceryneian Deer

Heracles' third task was to capture the Ceryneian deer. This was a swift, graceful female deer. She had golden horns.

Heracles tracked the animal for a year. He finally caught up with her by the Ladon River.

He did not wish to harm this beautiful creature. So he simply pinned her front legs together with one shot from his bow. Not a drop of blood was shed. Then he carried her to Eurystheus, who gave him his next assignment.

Labor 4: The Erymanthian Boar

Heracles was ordered to bring back the wild Erymanthian boar. Alive.

He hunted and hunted until he found the beast. It was living on Mount Erymanthus. And it was terrorizing the nearby villages.

Heracles chased it into a snowbank. Then he bound it with a heavy chain. He flung the boar over his shoulders and delivered it to Eurystheus.

Eurystheus was stunned. He was eager to find a labor that Heracles could not complete. So he dreamed up Heracles' fifth task.

Labor 5: The Stables of King Augeas

Heracles was commanded to clean out the stables of King Augeas. The king owned countless herds of cattle. And his stables were known to be filthy. After all, they had not been cleaned in over 20 years. The awful stench hung over the nearby mountains like a plague.

Eurystheus ordered Heracles to do the job in a single day. He provided him with one shovel and one basket.

"There!" exclaimed Eurystheus. "My dear cousin cannot rely on his strength alone for this. And I don't think he has the wits to think of a clever way out."

But Eurystheus was wrong. Heracles did think of a way. He picked up two rivers. And he set them down in the middle of the stable yard.

Soon, the whole area was clean!

Labor 6: The Stymphalian Birds

Eurystheus angrily ordered Heracles to confront a flock of flesh-eating birds. There were thousands of them. They lived in the Stymphalian Marsh.

They had long ruled the area. Many men had died trying to conquer them. The birds had brass daggers for feathers. And they shot them at all who dared to come near.

Well, Heracles tried to sneak up on the birds. But he was unable to move quickly through the marsh. He was just too heavy. He sank deeper with every step.

Luckily, his brother Hephaestus had given him some rattles. Heracles hid behind a rock and shook them wildly. He created a deafening racket. Then he watched as the birds squawked and flew away.

"I've frightened them off!" he cried.

The birds flew to the Isles of Ares in the Black Sea. And they never came back.

Labor 7: The Cretan Bull

Heracles next took on the Cretan bull. This beast was half man and half bull. It breathed fire. And it was destroying Crete's countryside.

This task proved simple for Heracles. He quickly won a violent struggle. Then he delivered the bull to Eurystheus.

Labor 8: The Mares of Diomedes

"Bring me the mares of Diomedes!" shouted Eurystheus. He was getting frustrated. He really didn't want Heracles to succeed.

Now these mares were known to eat men. So Heracles fed them the evil Diomedes. That was the horses' own master. This kept the mares busy while Heracles tied them up.

He dragged the whole herd to Eurystheus.

The king could not believe his eyes. But, of course, he did not wish to keep the mares.

So Heracles released them on Mount Olympus. And they were hunted and eaten by a horse-eating monster.

Labor 9: Hippolyte's Belt

Heracles was sent to the land of Queen Hippolyte. She ruled the Amazons. Somehow, Hippolyte had stolen Ares' magical belt. (Ares was the god of war.) Heracles' job was to steal the belt back.

But Eurystheus didn't count on Hippolyte cooperating with Heracles. At first glance, the queen fell in love with the hero. And she willingly handed over the belt!

Eurystheus had to quickly come up with yet another labor.

Labor 10: King Geryon's Cattle

King Geryon had three heads. And his guard had two. So Geryon's valuable herd of cattle was always under close watch. Heracles, as you might guess, was instructed to steal the cattle.

When Heracles arrived, Geryon's guard tried to stop him. But one blow from Heracles' club killed the guard instantly.

Then Geryon stormed at Heracles. And Heracles killed him with a single arrow through all three heads.

"What next?" Heracles asked.

Labor 11: Hera's Golden Apples

Upon seeing Geryon's cattle, Eurystheus thought for a moment. Finally, he laughed. He said, "I'm hungry for some apples."

Heracles knew that Eurystheus spoke of Hera's prized apples. You see, Hera owned a golden apple tree. And a deadly six-headed serpent guarded it for her.

"I'll get some for you," Heracles declared with confidence. "Then I will have but one labor left."

"*If* you can complete this one," sneered Eurystheus. "I demand that you get someone else to steal the apples. Otherwise, this labor will not count."

So Heracles set off. When he arrived at Hera's orchard, he studied the situation.

"I'd better take care of the snake first," he said. Then he struck each of the serpent's heads with a rock. The serpent was dead.

Heracles knew that Atlas was nearby. (He was supporting the earth on his shoulders.) So he went to him for help.

"Will you steal some apples for me, friend?" Heracles asked. "I can hold up the globe while you do it."

Atlas agreed. He really had no choice. Because he was holding up the earth as punishment for fighting Zeus. He could not turn down a request from Zeus's son!

Heracles' plan worked. And he took a bushel of golden apples back to Eurystheus.

Labor 12: The Capture of Cerberus

As his final labor, Heracles captured the beast Cerberus from Hades. Hades was the Land of the Dead. And no mortal had ever come back alive.

Heracles boarded the ferryboat to Hades. He crossed the river Styx. Soon, he was there—in the Land of the Dead.

During his voyage, Heracles had tricked the ghosts on the ferry. They had foolishly shown him how to get back. So after he throttled Cerberus, he rode the ferry home.

Eurystheus saw Cerberus's head. He was sad. But he was forced to admit—

"You are a true hero, Heracles. You have earned forgiveness. And your freedom. And one day, you shall take your rightful place among the gods."

And that's just what happened. The people and the gods celebrated Heracles' success. Heracles was granted eternal life. And he has been honored as a god ever since.

PANDORA'S BOX

ZEUS WAS VERY angry. The Titan Prometheus had tricked him into revealing the secret of fire. Then Prometheus had shared the secret with humankind.

"Prometheus shall pay for this!" vowed Zeus. "So shall humankind!"

And so Zeus hatched a plan. First, he took care of Prometheus. He chained him to a rock. And he sent a vulture to eat Prometheus's liver.

That night, the liver grew back. Then the vulture returned the next morning and ate it again. This went on—each day—for 30,000 years!

Next, Zeus created a girl out of clay. He named her Pandora. She was very sweet. And very beautiful.

"Charming," murmured Zeus. He was quite pleased with himself. Then he called a meeting of the gods.

"You shall each give Pandora a gift!" he announced. "See that it is a special one. For she is about to marry Epimetheus."

"Who is that?" asked Eros, the god of love.

"Epimetheus is Prometheus's brother," answered Zeus.

"And is Pandora meant to be with Epimetheus?"

"Indeed, Eros, indeed," said Zeus with a chuckle. "You might say Pandora was custom-made to be his bride."

Eros was satisfied. So he stepped forward and gave Pandora the gift of everlasting love.

Athene gave her the gift of wisdom. And she showed her how to spin and bake.

Poseidon gave her the key to the sea. And he promised that she would always be safe there.

Aphrodite gave her eternal beauty. And she taught her to dance.

Artemis taught her to hunt.

Demeter taught her to grow food and flowers.

And Apollo gave her the gift of music.

"These gifts are so lovely!" cried Pandora. "I don't know what to say!"

"But wait, my dear. There's more," said Hermes. He gave her a golden box. And he said, "This box is filled with glorious treasures. But you must never open it. If you do, you will be very sorry."

"I promise," said Pandora. "The box is so beautiful to look at. I shall never need to see inside." And she meant it.

At this point, Zeus gave Hera a nudge.

Hera said, "I have something for you too. From now on, you shall have the precious gift of curiosity."

"Thank you, Hera," said Pandora. "Thank you all."

With that, she was off to start her new life. Pandora didn't know that her marriage was just part of Zeus's scheme. So she lived quite happily. In fact, she did not suspect a thing. And neither did Epimetheus!

One day, Pandora and Epimetheus were walking through their lovely gardens. They talked about all the wonderful gifts Pandora had received.

"Which is your favorite?" Epimetheus asked.

"Oh, I could not choose," Pandora said. "All the gifts bring me such joy. Except . . ."

"Except what, my darling?"

"It's just that I sometimes wonder about the golden box. Hermes said that it contained 'glorious treasures.' Now why would he give me something like that and then tell me not to look inside?"

"I don't know," Epimetheus replied. "But I do think that you should follow his instructions. He is a god, you know. He probably had very good reasons. It's not for us to go against his wishes."

"You're right," agreed Pandora. "But don't you ever wonder what's under that lid?"

"Not really. Remember—you're the one with the great curiosity."

The couple continued to walk for a while in silence.

Zeus was watching from above. He flashed some lightning that only Epimetheus could see.

Epimetheus said suddenly, "I'm so sorry, dear. I just remembered something. I'm afraid that I must go on a journey. But I shall come back to you soon."

"Very well," said Pandora. "I shall miss you."

Epimetheus was gone in a matter of minutes. And Pandora was left alone with her thoughts. And the golden box.

"I can't stand it!" she said to a butterfly. "I simply must find out what's inside that box!"

So she went inside and took the box from its pedestal. She set it down on the floor. And she paced back and forth in front of it.

"Perhaps Hermes was playing a joke on me," she mused. "Why, I'll bet there's nothing at all inside. He's probably waiting for me to open it. So we can share a good laugh."

Then a dark thought came to her. "What if there's something evil inside? Like a deadly spider? Or a poison dart that's ready to pierce my heart?"

Pandora ran outside. She ran and ran until she was weak. She stopped to rest near a glistening brook. But thoughts of the golden box both haunted and thrilled her. So she made her way back home.

There she got down on her knees. She peered at the box for hours. She tried to will the lid to snap open on its own. But it did not.

At last, she undid the latch. She took a deep breath. And she opened the lid.

A flame shot up, but it died down just as quickly. Then out streamed a host of evils. Evils that man had never known. Disease and famine. Loss and deceit. Hatred and war. Pain and loss. Sadness and cruelty. And fear, suffering, and doubt.

Pandora screamed in agony. "What have I done! Oh, what have I done!"

She lunged at the box and slammed shut its lid. And it's a good thing she did. For one evil remained trapped inside.

That evil was *foreboding*. Had it been released, people would have had the ability to see into the future. They would know the misery that lay ahead. And there would be no hope left in the world.

Of course, Pandora did not know about foreboding. All she knew was that she had exposed people to countless ills. And she was deeply troubled.

Zeus soon showed up to gloat. "I see that you could not help yourself," he teased. "Things worked out splendidly!"

"So it was you!" cried Pandora. "You were behind this disaster!"

"Naturally," said Zeus. "I created you to teach Prometheus a lesson. It's simple, really. Humans cannot handle certain things.

"Take fire, for instance. If it had been left in the hands of the gods, everything would be in order. But Prometheus changed all that. Humans are already using it to destroy things—even each other. I decided it was time to show humans what else they'd been missing.

Now maybe they'll show the gods the respect they deserve!"

Pandora began to weep. She felt awful. "I cannot bear to live another day in this world!" she wailed. "Please, Zeus! End my suffering!"

"As you wish, Pandora," he said. "You've served your purpose."

Zeus gave two quick snaps of his fingers. Pandora turned back into a lump of clay at once. Zeus smiled and shook his head. Then he turned and walked away.

And he never looked back.

Long ago, Homer wrote the **Odyssey.** *The 12,000-line epic poem follows the heroic journey of Odysseus. The tale that follows focuses on some of Odysseus's most famous struggles.*

As the story opens, Odysseus has just fought a long and bloody war at Troy. Now all he wants to do is go home. He's been gone for ten years. He misses his beloved wife Penelope. And his son Telemachus.

Odysseus is a man of great courage and determination. He knows that he must get back to his family and the kingdom of Ithaca. And he will fight anyone who stands in his way. Even the gods.

The Return of Odysseus

The Long Journey Begins

IT WAS THE first day of the journey. And Odysseus's ship was caught in a terrible storm. It washed ashore. Odysseus and his men were in the Land of the Lotus-Eaters.

The sailors were hungry. So they ate some lotus fruit. But there was a problem. Anyone who ate the fruit wanted more. They could think of nothing else. And when they ate more, they wanted more still.

Odysseus tricked his men into coming back to the ship.

"Come back to the ship, men!" he called. "I have lots of lotus fruit for you. All you can eat. But it won't be there for long. Hurry up!"

The plan worked. And he sailed away from the fruit once and for all.

Next they sailed to Cyclopean Island. A one-eyed giant—a Cyclops—lived there.

The giant soon spotted Odysseus and his men. He lured them to his cave. Then he held them prisoner.

"You're mine now!" cried the Cyclops. "I'm going to take a walk. But I'll come back. And when I do, I'll be hungry!"

With that, the Cyclops closed off the entrance to his cave. The earth shook as he walked away.

"What is he going to do?" asked a sailor.

"He plans to have us for dinner," replied Odysseus. "We must come up with a plan. Otherwise, we'll never get out of here alive."

Odysseus continued. "All right, men. This

is what I know about Cyclopes. I know that they are stupid. And I know that they cannot feel pain. If we can blind this one, I think we can get away safely."

When the Cyclops returned, he yawned. And he said, "All this trapping has made me sleepy. So I'm going to take a nap. When I awake, I'll let my sheep out to graze. Then— it's dinnertime for me!"

"Perfect!" whispered Odysseus.

The second the Cyclops fell asleep, Odysseus sprang into action. He stabbed the giant's eye with a spear.

When the giant awoke, he didn't notice his blindness. He just stumbled his way around the cave.

"Come on, sheep," he cooed. "Time for you to graze."

As the sheep went out, the men each held on to a sheep's belly. They passed right by the unsuspecting giant. In moments, they were back on their ship. And the Cyclops had forgotten all about them!

Now one day, the Cyclops had a visitor. It was another, smarter Cyclops. And he had heard rumors of Odysseus's trick.

This second giant explained to the first that he had been tricked. And the first became very angry. He was so angry that he asked Poseidon to punish Odysseus.

Poseidon was the god of the sea. The Cyclops had once done him a favor. So he agreed to steer Odysseus's ship off course. This added years to the trip.

Odysseus Continues His Voyage

During those years, Odysseus faced many struggles. For example, the witch Circe turned some of his men into pigs. And she held Odysseus prisoner for a while.

"Stay with me forever," Circe begged.

But Odysseus still wanted to be with Penelope. "Nothing will keep me from her," he said. And Circe let him go.

Later, Odysseus and his men had to travel through the Strait of the Sirens. The Sirens were part pixie, part female. They sang lovely, bewitching songs. But if they drew you near, they'd eat you.

Luckily, Circe had given Odysseus a spell. He cast it over his men. It kept them from being tempted by the Sirens. He also filled their ears with beeswax. Just to be safe.

But Odysseus himself was very curious. He wanted to hear the Sirens' song. So he had his men tie him to the boat. That way, he could listen to the music. But he could not break free and go to the Sirens. No matter how tempted he was.

Next, the men had to sail past Scylla. She was a ferocious six-headed monster. She killed two of the sailors. But Odysseus and the others survived.

As his ship sailed to Aiaia, Odysseus received a warning. It was from Circe. She told him not to eat the island's cattle.

"But my men are starving," he said. "I see no choice. They must eat."

And so they did. The gods punished the men by sinking the ship. Odysseus was the only survivor. He held on to the ship's mast for days. He finally washed ashore on Calypso's island.

Calypso was a powerful nymph. Like Circe, she wanted Odysseus to stay with her. But Odysseus refused.

"I must get home," he explained.

Calypso said, "Ah, but you have no choice. I have the power to keep you here." She did so for seven long years.

Odysseus was miserable. "I miss my home and my wife!" he bellowed one day. "Who are you to keep me against my will?"

"Don't you see?" replied Calypso. "This is

my island. *My* will is the only one that matters. Besides, you amuse me."

Just then, Zeus appeared. He said, "You are being selfish, Calypso. Let him go."

"But I want him to stay," she pouted.

"I know," he said. "But surely you could find someone else to fall in love with. Aren't you getting bored with a mere mortal?"

"Now that you mention it," she said, "perhaps I am. Why, I should be looking for a powerful wizard. Or even a god."

"Then it is settled," said Zeus. "Odysseus shall return home at once."

Ithaca at Last!

Odysseus was given a new ship. He sailed home swiftly. Soon, he saw his beloved Ithaca on the horizon. He was overjoyed.

He docked his ship and headed straight for home. But then something hit him—

Nobody there knew what had become of him. Nobody knew of his valiant struggle to come home.

He told himself, "For all they know, I abandoned them. Or perhaps they think I am dead. After all, it has been 20 years."

Odysseus did not want to shock his family too much. So he disguised himself as an old beggar.

"I'll visit the palace like this. Perhaps I can learn what they think of me."

Odysseus lurked around his courtyard for a while. There was much activity. Everyone was preparing for a big celebration.

Odysseus spotted a maid he remembered. She was a kind soul. When she saw the old beggar, she waved him over.

"Here," she said. "Take these." She held out a jug of water and some bread. "We have more than enough here."

"Thank you," Odysseus said, bowing. "Your kindness shall not go unrewarded."

The maid laughed and said, "Don't worry about it. We can all use a helping hand now and then."

"Tell me, if you will, what is going on here today?"

"There's going to be a wedding," replied the maid. "The nobles are forcing Penelope to remarry. So she is holding a contest. The winner shall be her new husband."

"What type of contest?"

"All suitors must try to string her dead husband's bow. The one who succeeds and shoots an arrow will be her choice."

"Her husband's dead, you say?"

"Yes," answered the maid sadly. "He was

lost at sea. He was a brave, good man. And Penelope loved him with all her heart."

The maid went on. "If you ask me, she does not wish to remarry. So I think she's hoping that no one can string Odysseus's bow. It's a very difficult task. It calls for an exceptionally skilled archer."

"So I've arrived just in time," noted Odysseus.

"What?" The maid was a bit baffled by his remark.

"For the contest, I mean. May I watch?" Odysseus asked.

"You may—if you stay out of the way," she said.

"I thank you again."

"You're welcome," said the maid brightly. "Now I must get back to my duties. See that you eat that bread. And see that you don't cause any trouble."

"On my honor," he said.

The Contest

The noble guests gathered to watch the contest. Penelope entered the courtyard. She explained the rules to her suitors. Each one would try to string the bow. Then he would send an arrow through a distant row of 12 axes. The axes should remain standing—with the arrow binding them together.

Penelope offered the bow to the first man in line. And the contest began.

Odysseus watched from his spot near a fig tree. Soon, a young man approached him.

"Tell me, old man. What do you make of the contest?"

"It's very interesting," said Odysseus. "I hope you don't mind my watching."

"Not at all," replied the young fellow. "I saw the maid giving you some bread. Did you get enough?"

"Quite," said Odysseus. "Are you one of the suitors?"

The young man laughed. "I should think not! Penelope is my mother!"

"Telemachus?" Odysseus gasped.

"How do you know my name?"

"Follow me," commanded Odysseus. "I must talk to you."

Telemachus followed. But he was becoming suspicious of the beggar.

Odysseus led his son away from the crowd. Then he announced, "I am your father— Odysseus. I have returned. I fought in the Trojan War. And I've been battling the raging sea for ten years."

"That's impossible!" cried Telemachus. "One of my father's sailors reported to my mother. He saw my father drown."

"That sailor was a fake," declared Odysseus. "All my men were killed. Penelope's advisers must have paid someone to lie. They always wanted to get their hands on my money."

Telemachus was shocked. But he was happy. He so wanted to believe that his father—the great hero—had returned.

"Come," he said. "I must take you to my mother."

"Let's see how the contest ends before we talk to her. I have a plan."

"Very well," said Telemachus. "But if you are lying to me, I shall have your head."

The Happy Reunion

Father and son returned to the courtyard. The last suitor was trying to string the bow. He failed. As had each man before him.

Penelope addressed the crowd. "There will be no wedding today. For no one can replace my Odysseus. But please—stay and eat. We shall have a party in my husband's memory."

Just as the music began, Odysseus stepped forward. He was still disguised as the beggar.

"Dear lady!" he boomed. The sound of his powerful voice stopped the music. All eyes turned to him. And he continued—

"I should like a chance to string the bow."

Penelope's eyes sparkled. She liked bold people. "All right," she said. "My guests and I would enjoy the spectacle. But you do understand that you are not a possible husband for me."

"I understand much more than you think, milady. Let me string the bow. Then whatever happens between us shall be your decision."

The guests were aghast. A common beggar had spoken fearlessly to Penelope! They whispered among themselves heatedly.

"The nerve!" said one.

"Who *is* that man?" asked another.

"He should be thrown out!" declared a third.

Penelope silenced the crowd. And she handed Odysseus the bow.

Odysseus easily strung it. He took aim for the briefest moment. And he sent an arrow directly to the target. It passed cleanly through the ax handles.

Telemachus rushed forward. He shouted, "Father!"

Odysseus threw off his disguise. And he took an astonished Penelope in his arms.

"Odysseus—my love!" she cried. "You have come back to me!"

"In my heart, I never left," he proclaimed.

Odysseus, Penelope, and Telemachus were reunited at last.

The crowd roared with excitement. This was the biggest news to hit Ithaca in 20 years. Soon, the people were chanting—

"Odysseus! Odysseus! Long live Odysseus!"

A grand celebration followed. And the legend of Odysseus's return lived on forever.

The Return of Odysseus

The Play

Cast of Characters

Narrator	Calypso
Odysseus	Zeus
Cyclops 1	Palace Maid
Sailor	Telemachus
Cyclops 2	Penelope
Poseidon	Guest 1
Circe	Guest 2
The Sirens	Guest 3
(3 female voices)	Crowd
Scylla	(10–15 voices)

Setting: A journey by sea from Troy to Ithaca long ago

Act I

Narrator: Odysseus fought a long and bloody war at Troy. When it was over, all he wanted to do was go home. He'd been away from Ithaca for ten years. He missed his beloved wife Penelope. And his son Telemachus.

But his journey was filled with danger.

First, his ship was caught in a terrible storm. It washed ashore. Odysseus and his men had come to the Land of the Lotus-Eaters.

The sailors were hungry. So they ate some lotus fruit. But there was a problem. Anyone who ate the fruit wanted more. They could think of nothing else. And when they ate more, they wanted more still.

Luckily, Odysseus noticed this before he ate the fruit. And he came up with an idea.

Odysseus: Come back to the ship, men. I have lots of lotus fruit for you. All you can eat. But it won't be there for long. Hurry up!

Narrator: Odysseus's plan worked. His men boarded the ship. And he sailed them away from the fruit once and for all.

Then they sailed to Cyclopean Island. A one-eyed giant—a Cyclops—lived there.

The giant soon spotted Odysseus and his men. He lured them to his cave. Then he held them prisoner.

Cyclops 1: You're mine now! I'm going out for a while. But I'll come back. And when I do, I'll be hungry!

Narrator: The Cyclops closed off the cave's entrance. The earth shook as he walked away.

Sailor: What is he going to do?

Odysseus: He plans to have us for dinner. We must come up with a plan. Otherwise, we'll never get out of here alive.

All right, men. This is what I know about Cyclopes. I know that they are stupid. And I know that they cannot feel pain. If we can blind this one, I think we can get away safely.

Narrator: Later, the Cyclops returned. He yawned.

Cyclops 1: All this trapping has made me sleepy. So I'm going to take a nap. When I awake, I'll let my sheep out to graze. Then— it's dinnertime for me!

Odysseus: Perfect!

Cyclops 1: What did you say?

Odysseus: Nothing, sir. Have a nice nap.

Narrator: The Cyclops fell asleep. And Odysseus sprang into action. He stabbed the giant's eye with a spear.

When the giant awoke, he didn't notice his blindness. He just stumbled his way around the cave.

Cyclops 1: Come on, sheep. Time for you to graze.

Narrator: As the sheep went out, each man held on to a sheep's belly. They passed right by the unsuspecting giant. In moments, they were back on their ship. And the Cyclops had forgotten all about them!

But one day, the Cyclops had a visitor. It was another, smarter Cyclops.

Cyclops 2: I've heard rumors. It seems that you were tricked by Odysseus. He made you look like a fool.

Cyclops 1: I will not stand for that! Poseidon! Where are you?

Narrator: Poseidon was the god of the sea. The Cyclops had once done him a favor. So he answered the Cyclops.

Poseidon: What can I do for you?

Cyclops 1: Odysseus has mocked me. Now he must pay. Will you help?

Poseidon: Yes. I can steer Odysseus's ship off course. This will add many years to his trip.

Cyclops 1: Good. Do it right away.

Act II

Narrator: During the next few years, Odysseus faced many struggles. For example, the witch Circe turned some of his men into pigs. And she kept Odysseus on her island for a while. She didn't want to release him.

Circe: Stay with me forever, Odysseus.

Odysseus: I've told you. Nothing will keep me from Penelope.

Circe: Go if you must. But be careful.

Narrator: Later, Odysseus and his men traveled through the Strait of the Sirens. Sirens were part pixie, part female. They sang lovely, bewitching songs. Their aim was to draw people near—so they could eat them.

Luckily, Circe had given Odysseus a spell. He cast it over his men. It kept them from being tempted by the Sirens. He also filled their ears with beeswax. Just to be safe.

But Odysseus himself was very curious.

Odysseus: Tie me to the boat, men. That way, I can listen to the music. But I will not be able to break free and go to the Sirens. No matter how much they tempt me.

Narrator: The men did as they were told.

The Sirens: Come to us, Odysseus. Come to us, Odysseus. It's lovely here! The breeze is soft. And the water is warm . . .

Odysseus: Let me go, men! I want to go to the Sirens.

Narrator: But his men followed his earlier orders. They ignored him. And the boat passed safely through the strait.

Next, they had to sail past Scylla. She was a ferocious six-headed monster. She killed two of the sailors. But Odysseus and the others survived.

Scylla: I'll get you, too, Odysseus—if you dare to come back!

Narrator: As his ship sailed to Aiaia, Odysseus received a warning. It was from Circe.

Circe: Whatever you do, do not to eat the island's cattle. It will only bring you misery.

Odysseus: But my men are starving. I see no choice. They must eat.

Narrator: And so they did. The gods punished the men by sinking the ship. Odysseus was the only survivor. He held on to the ship's mast for days. He finally washed ashore on Calypso's island.

Calypso was a powerful nymph. Like Circe, she wanted Odysseus to stay with her. But Odysseus refused.

Odysseus: I must get home.

Calypso: Ah, but you have no choice. I have the power to keep you here.

Narrator: She did so for seven long years. Odysseus was miserable.

Odysseus: I miss my home and my wife! Who are you to keep me against my will?

Calypso: Don't you see? This is my island. My will is the only one that matters. Besides, you amuse me.

Narrator: Just then, Zeus appeared.

Zeus: You are being selfish, Calypso. Let him go.

Calypso: But I want him to stay.

Zeus: I know. But surely you could find someone else to fall in love with. Aren't you getting bored with a mere mortal?

Calypso: Now that you mention it, perhaps I am. Why, I should be looking for a powerful wizard. Or even a god.

Zeus: Then it is settled. Odysseus shall return home at once.

<u>Act III</u>

Narrator: Odysseus was given a new ship. He sailed home swiftly. Soon, he saw his beloved Ithaca on the horizon. He was overjoyed.

He docked his ship and headed straight for home. But then something hit him. Nobody there knew what had become of him. Nobody knew of his valiant struggle to come home.

Odysseus: For all they know, I abandoned them. Or perhaps they think I am dead. After all, it has been 20 years.

Narrator: Odysseus did not want to shock his family too much. So he disguised himself as an old beggar.

Odysseus: I'll visit the palace like this. Perhaps I can learn what they think of me.

Narrator: Odysseus lurked around his courtyard for a while. There was much activity. Everyone was preparing for a big celebration.

Odysseus spotted a maid he remembered. She was a kind soul. When she saw the old beggar, she waved him over. She held out a jug of water and some bread.

Palace Maid: Here. Take these. We have more than enough here.

Odysseus: Thank you. Your kindness shall not go unrewarded.

Palace Maid: Don't worry about it. We can all use a helping hand now and then.

Odysseus: Tell me, if you will, what is going on here today?

Palace Maid: There's going to be a wedding. The nobles are forcing Penelope to remarry. So she is holding a contest. The winner shall be her new husband.

Odysseus: What type of contest?

Palace Maid: All suitors must try to string her dead husband's bow. The one who succeeds and shoots an arrow will be her choice.

Odysseus: Her husband's dead, you say?

Palace Maid: Yes. He was lost at sea. He was a brave, good man. And Penelope loved him with all her heart.

If you ask me, she does not wish to remarry. So I think she's hoping that no one can string Odysseus's bow. It's a very difficult task. It calls for an exceptionally skilled archer.

Odysseus: So I've arrived just in time.

Palace Maid: What do you mean?

Odysseus: For the contest, of course. May I watch?

Palace Maid: You may—if you stay out of the way.

Odysseus: I thank you again.

Palace Maid: You're welcome. Now I must get back to my duties. See that you eat that bread. And see that you don't cause any trouble.

Odysseus: On my honor.

Act IV

Narrator: The noble guests gathered to watch the contest. Penelope entered the courtyard. She explained the rules to her suitors.

Penelope: Each one of you shall try to string the bow. Then you should send an arrow through that distant row of 12 axes. The axes should remain standing—with the arrow binding them together.

Narrator: Penelope offered the bow to the first man in line. And the contest began.

Odysseus watched from his spot near a fig tree. Soon, a young man approached him.

Telemachus: Tell me, old man. What do you make of the contest?

Odysseus: It's very interesting. I hope you don't mind my watching.

Telemachus: Not at all. I saw the maid giving you some bread. Did you get enough?

Odysseus: Quite. Are you one of the suitors?

Telemachus: I should think not! Penelope is my mother!

Narrator: Odysseus gasped.

Odysseus: Telemachus?

Telemachus: How do you know my name?

Odysseus: Follow me. I must talk to you.

Narrator: Telemachus followed. But he was becoming suspicious of the beggar.
Odysseus led his son away from the crowd. Then he announced—

Odysseus: I am your father—Odysseus. I have returned. I fought in the Trojan War. And I've been battling the raging sea ever since.

Telemachus: That's impossible! One of my father's sailors reported to my mother. He saw my father drown.

Odysseus: That sailor was a fake. All my men were killed. Penelope's advisers must have paid someone to lie. They always wanted to get their hands on my money.

Narrator: Telemachus was shocked. But he was happy. He so wanted to believe that his father had returned.

Telemachus: Come—I must take you to my mother.

Odysseus: Let's see how the contest ends before we talk to her. I have a plan.

Telemachus: Very well. But if you are lying to me, I shall have your head.

Act V

Narrator: Father and son returned to the courtyard. The last suitor was trying to string the bow. He failed. As had each man before him.

Penelope addressed the crowd.

Penelope: There will be no wedding today. For no one can replace my Odysseus. But please—stay and eat. We shall have a party in my husband's memory.

Narrator: Just as the music began,

Odysseus stepped forward. He was still disguised as the beggar. The sound of his powerful voice stopped the music.

Odysseus: Dear lady!

Narrator: All eyes turned to him.

Odysseus: I should like a chance to string the bow.

Narrator: Penelope's eyes sparkled. She liked bold people.

Penelope: All right. My guests and I would enjoy the spectacle. But you do understand that you are not a possible husband for me.

Odysseus: I understand much more than you think, milady. Let me string the bow. Then whatever happens between us shall be your decision.

Narrator: The guests were aghast. A common beggar had spoken fearlessly to Penelope! They whispered among themselves heatedly.

Guest 1: The nerve!

Guest 2: Who is that man?

Guest 3: He should be thrown out!

Penelope: Silence!

Narrator: Penelope handed Odysseus the bow. Odysseus easily strung it. He took aim for the briefest moment. And he sent an arrow directly to the target. It passed cleanly through the ax handles.

Telemachus rushed forward.

Telemachus: Father!

Narrator: Odysseus threw off his disguise. And he took an astonished Penelope in his arms.

Penelope: Odysseus—my love! You have come back to me!

Odysseus: In my heart, I never left.

Narrator: Odysseus, Penelope, and Telemachus were reunited at last.

The crowd roared with excitement. This was the biggest news to hit Ithaca in 20 years. Soon, the people were chanting.

Crowd: Odysseus! Odysseus! Long live Odysseus!

Narrator: A grand celebration followed. And the legend of Odysseus's return lived on forever.